Copyright 2020 - by Beth Costanzo

Leopards are some of the most beautiful and deadly creatures on our planet. While other cats (like lions and tigers) may get more attention, leopards are extremely fascinating animals.

You may be able to see leopards in your local zoo. If you're lucky, you may even see them in the wild. But whether you are seeing a leopard in person or simply looking at a picture of them on the Internet, there are plenty of fun facts to learn. Let's explore some of those fun facts right now!

Leopards

ADVENTURESOFSCUBAJACK.COM

When looking at an animal like a leopard, it's useful to first learn some facts about its physical makeup. The leopard is widely known for its distinctive black spots. These dark spots are gathered in groups called *rosettes*. Along with its black spots, the leopard has a skin color that ranges from a pale yellow color to a dark golden color. It also has a white belly.

Leopards are fairly large creatures. Males are larger than females. Leopards' head and body length are approximately 35 to 77 inches long. Leopards also have large tails, which measure around 26 to 40 inches long. The heaviest leopard found in the wild weighed about 212 pounds, but male leopards, in general, weigh around 175 pounds. Leopards generally live to be about 12 to 17 years old.

Besides its height and weight, one of the most fascinating things about the leopard is its speed. When they are sprinting, leopards can reach top speeds of around 36 miles per hour. Their speed comes in handy when they are hunting their prey. Leopards are carnivores, meaning that they eat meat. Leopards tend to hunt at night and like to find prey that weighs between 22 and 88 pounds. Some of the animals that they like to eat include impala, bushbuck, chital, and even giraffes.

Leopards are known to be extremely patient hunters. They stalk their prey and try to attack it when they are as close as possible. It often pounces on its prey by biting it on the neck or by jumping on its face and killing its prey through suffocation. Once it kills its prey, the leopard tends to bring its food up a tree. You definitely don't want to get in their way when they are hunting!

Leopards don't have many natural predators. They can live peacefully with other large predators like tigers, hyenas, lions, and cheetahs. That said, Nile crocodiles and sloth bears have attacked leopards in the past. The same is true of lions and tigers. As is the case with many large animals, however, humans represent one of the biggest threats to leopards. Along with the destruction of their habitats, humans have hunted leopards.

From prey and predators, let's talk about where you can find leopards in the wild. They are often found in Africa and Asia. Specifically, you can find them in countries like South Africa, Sri Lanka, Thailand, Malaysia, Indonesia, and Laos. As you can tell, leopards like living in warmer climates. They feel at home in the savannah and rainforest.

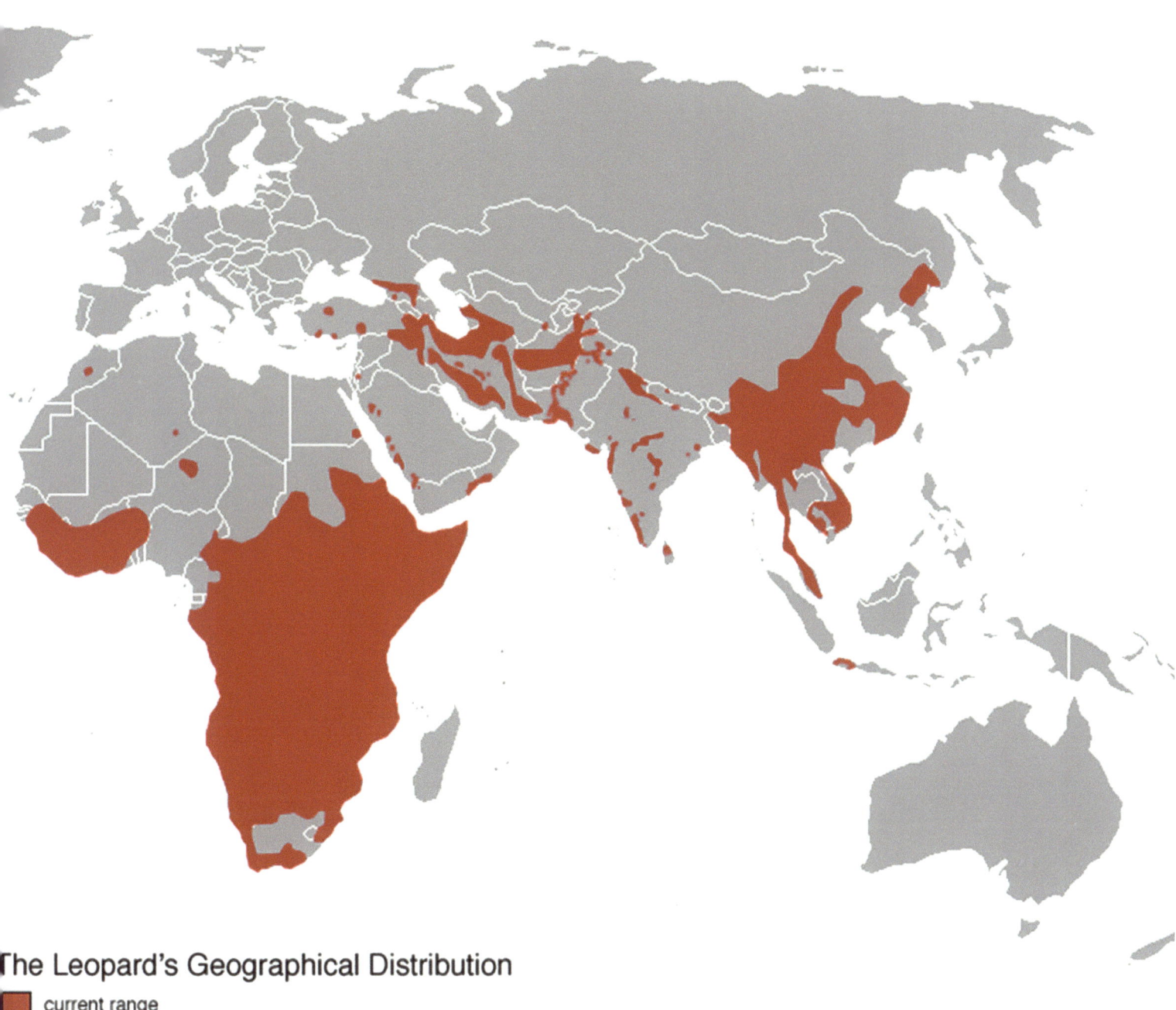

The Leopard's Geographical Distribution
current range

Unfortunately, you can't see leopards in the wild in the United States or in other North American countries. Some zoos have them, however, so you'll want to double check before visiting your local zoo.

Now, let's talk about one of the cutest things that you can see in the wild: baby leopards. It depends on where they are located, but some leopards have children all year round. When female leopards are ready to give birth, they often do it in a cave, hollow tree, crevice among rocks, or in a thicket. In leopard cubs' first moments of life, they have closed eyes. Their eyes remain closed for as long as four to nine days! Cubs are often born in a litter of two to four cubs, so they will have plenty of company when they are born.

How Jaguars Are Similar to Leopards

When looking at the leopard, you may confuse them with another awesome animal: the jaguar. It would be easy to make that mistake. Jaguars and leopards look very similar. Both animals are cats and they have distinctive spots.

There are also some other similarities between leopards and jaguars. For example, both leopards and jaguars are ferocious hunters. They are muscular and ambush their prey when they least expect it.

However, there are some differences. Most notably, the jaguar is bigger and more robust than the leopard. Jaguars are the biggest cats in their habitat (Central America and South America) while leopards are some of the smaller cats in their habitat. Jaguars are also more arrogant than leopards. They know that they're the king of the jungle and they act like it. On the other hand, leopards are a little more scrappy.

There are plenty more differences. However, the most important comes down to appearance. So the next time you are looking at a spotted animal, look at its size. Leopards are smaller than jaguars, so keep that in mind when you are looking through your binoculars.

9 Types of Leopards

ADVENTURESOFSCUBAJACK.COM

Sri Lankan Leopard

Javen Leopard

Indo Chinese Leopard

Amur Leopard

North Chinese Leopard

Persian Leopard

Arabian Leopard

Indian Leopard

African Leopard

Simply put, leopards are fascinating creatures. They roam habitats like rainforests and are extremely patient when searching for food. In fact, they may become your new favorite animal.

In case you are looking for more information about leopards, here are some more fun facts.

• The oldest recorded leopard was a female named Roxanne. She lived to be 24 years, 2 months, and 13 days old.

• The earliest known leopard fossils were found in Europe. These fossils are about 600,000 years old.

• Leopards can jump 20 feet horizontally and around 10 feet vertically. This helps them when they need to catch prey or climb up trees.

• Male leopards consume around 8 pounds of food per day while females consume around 6 pounds.

• Leopards have been featured in mythology, art, and folklore throughout human history.

• The leopard's pupils are round.

• The African leopard is the most widespread leopard subspecies in the world.

• The whitish spots on the back of leopards' ears are thought to play a role in communication.

Leopards Activities

TRACING

Trace the word then write it

ADVENTURESOFSCUBAJACK.COM

MAZE

Help the female leopard to find her 3 cubs

COUNTING

Circle the correct answer

7 8 9	7 6 5
7 6 8	4 6 5

Leopard Craft

ADVENTURESOFSCUBAJACK.COM

Let's make a leopard together!

You will need:

Scissors
Glue
Marker Pen or Pencil
Coloring Pencils

Directions:

1- Cut the body, head, back legs with the sissors
2- Glue the back legs to the body
3- Glue the head to the body
4- Draw the nose and the mouth of the leopard
5- Draw the leopard pattern
6- Color your leopard

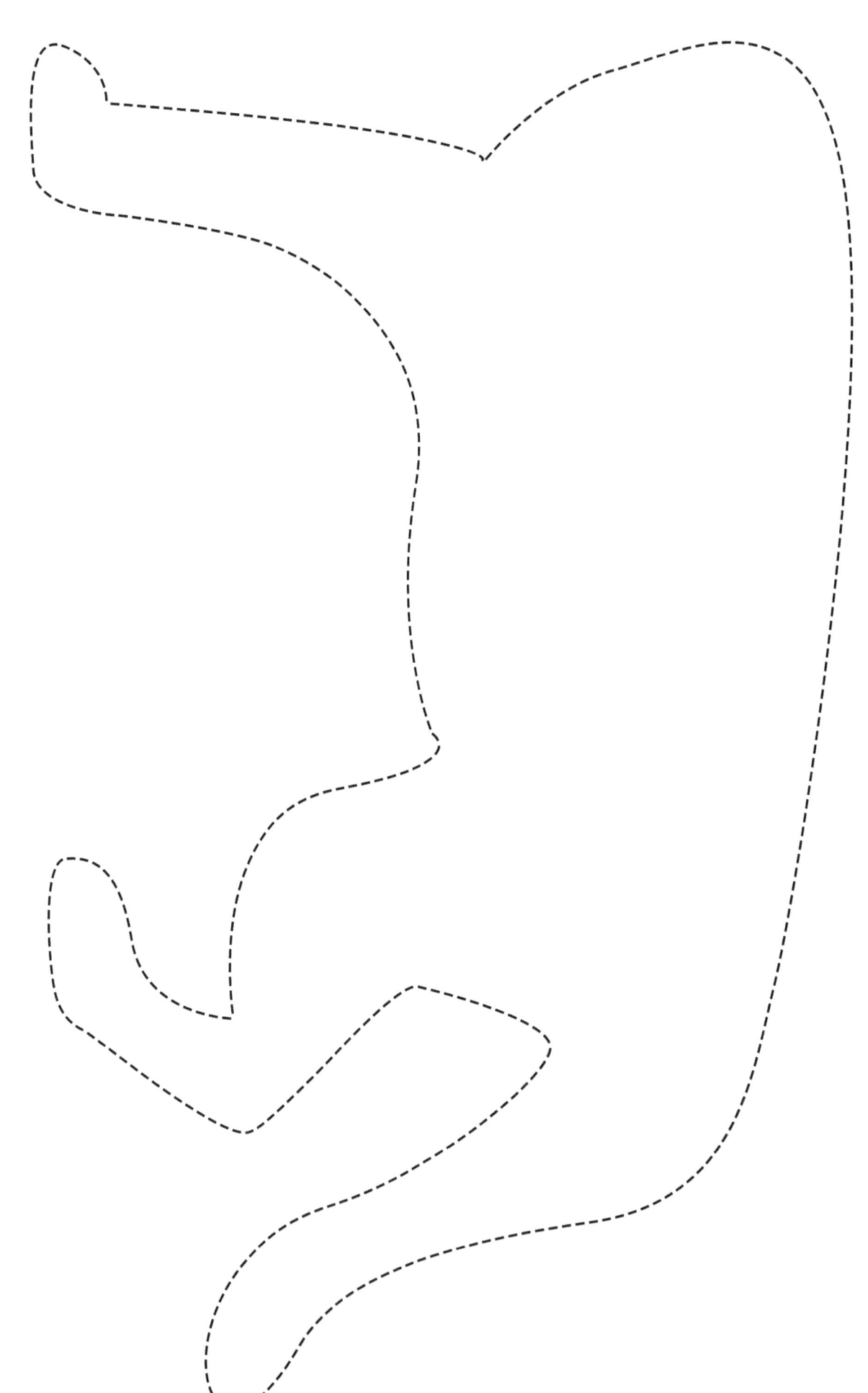

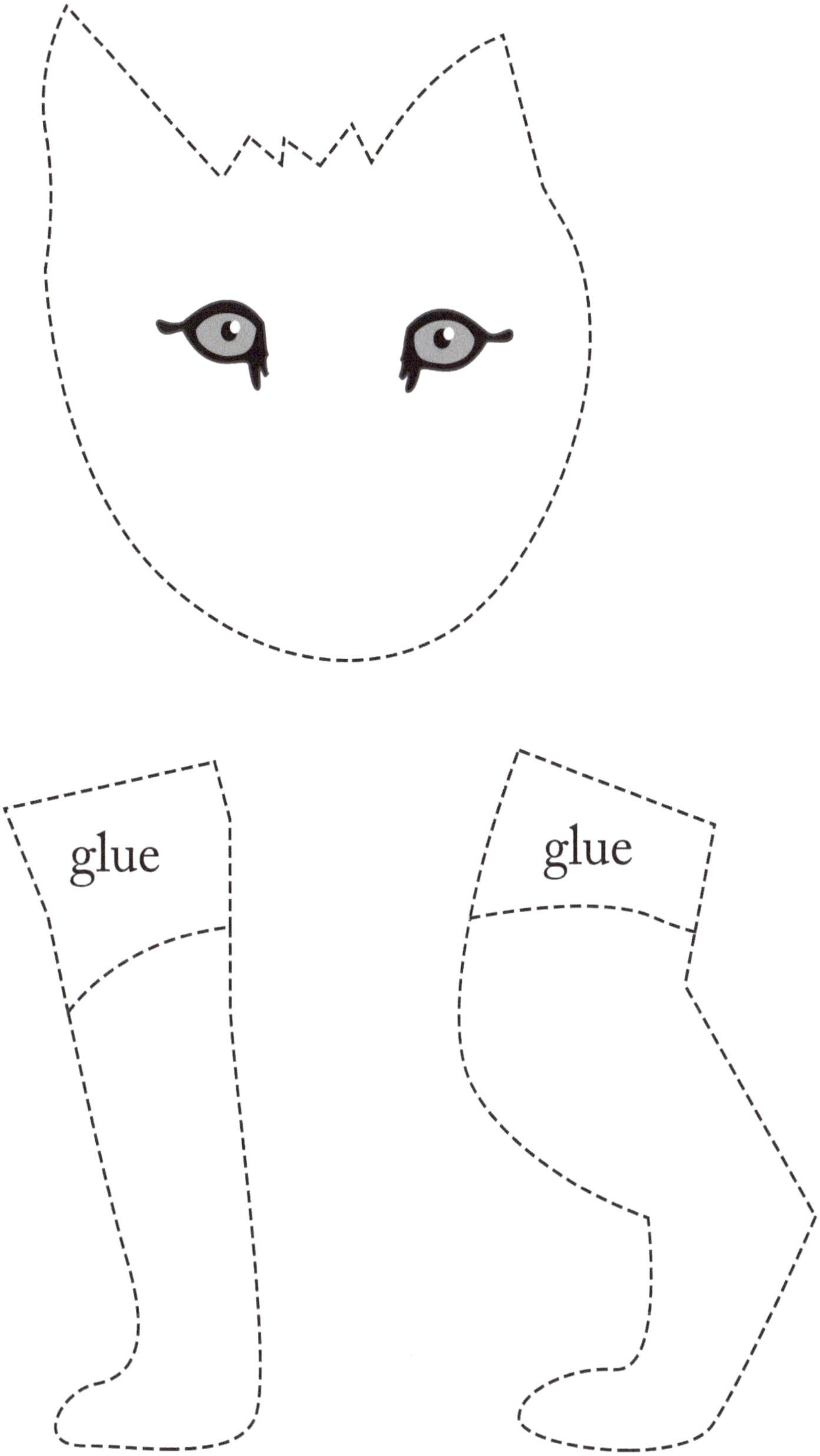

glue   glue

ADVENTURESOFSCUBAJACK.COM

Visit us at:

www.adventuresofscubajack.com

www.ingramcontent.com/pod-product-compliance
Lightning Source LLC
Chambersburg PA
CBHW041436010526
44118CB00002B/84